Pun and Games

TIME'S FUN W

RE HAVING FLIES

and

Games

Jokes, riddles, daffynitions, tairy fales, rhymes, and more wordplay for kids

Richard Lederer

Illustrated by Dave Morice

CHICAGO
REVIEW
PRESS

Library of Congress Cataloging-in-Publication Data

Lederer, Richard, 1938-
Pun and games : jokes, riddles, daffynitions, tairy fales, rhymes, and more
  wordplay for kids / Richard Lederer : illustrated by Dave Morice. —
  1st ed.
          p.   cm.
Summary: An introduction to wordplay, including puns, spoonerisms,
  riddles, and more.
          ISBN 1-55652-264-9
  1. Puns and punning.   2. Riddles, Juvenile. 3. Word games.
  [1. Puns and punning.   2. Riddles. 3. Word games.] I. Morice, Dave,
1946-   ill.   II. Title.
  PN6231.P8L43   1996   96-11609
  793.73—dc20   CIP
                                              AC

©1996 by Richard Lederer
Illustrations ©1996 by Dave Morice
The poem entitled "A Bazaar Tale" (see chapter 8) is reprinted with the
permission of Simon & Schuster from *The Miracle of Language* by Richard
Lederer.©1991 by Richard Lederer.
Published by Chicago Review Press, Incorporated
814 North Franklin Street
Chicago, Illinois 60610
ISBN 1-55652-264-9
Printed in the United States of America
5 4

To John S. Crosbie,
Chairman of the Bored of
the International Save the Pun Foundation,

to the once and future grandchildren
of Richard Lederer,

and to Danny Morice

Contents

1 It's a Punderful Life 1

2 Homographs at Play 9

3 Calling on the Homophone 19

4 Double Plays 25

5 Have You Ever Seen a Home Run? 33

6 Four Cheers Five Inflationary Language 39

7 "Let's Play a Game," Said Tom Swiftly 43

8 A Bazaar Tale 49

9 Licensed 2 Pun 53

10 Puns That Babylon 59

11 Pun Your Way to Success 65

12 A Daffynitions Fictionary 71

13 Furry Tells end Noisier Rams 77

14 Silver Spoonerisms 83

15 What's the Difference? 91

16 Tairy Fales 97

Pun and Games

It's a Punderful Life

Fuzzy Wuzzy wasn't fuzzy, was he?

anguage is fun. Everyone who speaks and listens and reads and writes is involved with the natural playfulness of language. Much of that play takes the form of punning, as in this verse, which has fun with the two meanings of the word *weather* and its similarity in sound to *whether:*

> *Whether the weather is good,*
> *Or whether the weather is not;*
> *Whether the weather is cold,*
> *Or whether the weather is hot;*

1

> *We'll weather the weather,*
> *Whatever the weather,*
> *Whether we like it or not!*

You have been speaking, hearing, and reading puns most of your life. When you were very young, you probably chanted songs like

> *Fuzzy Wuzzy was a bear.*
> *Fuzzy Wuzzy had no hair.*
> *Fuzzy Wuzzy wasn't fuzzy, was he?*

and

> *A sailor went to C-C-C,*
> *To see what he could C-C-C,*
> *But all that he could C-C-C*
> *Was the bottom of a great blue C-C-C.*

These verses are children's first attempts to put into memorable form their pleasure in discovering that the same sound can suggest two or three different meanings—*Wuzzy* and *was he; C, sea,* and *see.*

Words and sounds that spark forth two or more meanings are called puns. A pun has been defined as a play upon words, a play upun words, and a prey upon words.

Unless you were raised as a hermit (or, if you are a boy, a hismit), you probably recognize many of these traditional riddles:

What's black and white and red (read) all over?
> *A newspaper.*

What did the letter say to the stamp?
Stick with me and we'll go places.

What kind of shoes are made from banana skins?
Slippers.

What kind of rooms have no walls?
Mushrooms.

How do you know when it's raining cats and dogs?
When you step in a poodle.

How do you know when it's raining cats and dogs?

When is a door not a door?
When it's ajar.

What happened to the boy who drank 8 Cokes?
He burped 7-Up.

Pun Fun

Here's a game riddled with *pun*ch lines. Guess the punch lines to these popular Silly Billy jokes. You'll find the answers to all questions in this book at the end of each chapter.

1. Why did Silly Billy throw the clock out the window?
   He wanted to see time _____.

2. Why did Silly Billy throw the butter out the window?
   He wanted to see butter _____.

3. Why did Silly Billy take a ladder to the ball park?
   He wanted to see the _____ play.

4. Why did Silly Billy tiptoe past the medicine cabinet?
   He didn't want to wake up the _____ pills.

5. Why did Silly Billy jump off the Empire State Building?
   He wanted to make a _____ _____ on Broadway.

Now, without any clues, try to guess the answers to these elephant jokes:

6. Where do elephants store their clothes?

7. How do you make an elephant float?

8. What happens to a grape when an elephant steps on it?

9. How can you stop an elephant from charging?

10. Who are the two most famous elephant singers?

Here are fifteen posters and placards that have appeared around the world. They are all signs of our times, times in which we human beings love to fiddle with words and to laugh at the loony tunes that such fiddling produces:

At a tire store: Time to re-tire.

Over a display of batteries: Wanna start something?

In a music store window: Guitars for sale. Cheap. No strings attached.

In a pet store window: Merry Christmas and a Yappy New Year.

On a peanut stand: If our peanuts were any fresher, they'd be insulting.

In an ice cream and dairy store: You can't beat our milk shakes, but you can whip our cream and lick our ice-cream cones.

In a shoe store: Come in and have a fit.

In a real estate office: Get lots for little.

In a butcher shop window: Never a bum steer.

At a poultry farm: Better laid than ever.

On a southern street: No U-all turns.

Over a bargain basement counter: What you seize is what you get.

In a beauty parlor: Curl up and dye.

In a restaurant: Don't stand outside and be miserable. Come inside and be fed up.

In a delicatessen: Protect your bagels. Put lox on them.

Lighten up your garden. Plant _____.

Pun Fun

Here are ten more real signs. Supply the missing words.

11. *On a diaper service truck:* Rock a _____ baby.

12. *At a planetarium:* Cast of thousands. Every one a _____.

13. *On the wall of a dentist's office:* Always be true to your teeth, or they will be _____ to you.

14. *Outside an optician's shop:* _____ for sore eyes.

15. *In the window of a watch repair shop:* If it doesn't tick, _____ to us.

16. *In a jewelry store:* There's no present like the _____.

17. *In a billiard parlor window:* Try our indoor _____.

18. *At a tire store:* We _____ you not.

19. *In a garden shop:* Lighten up your garden. Plant _____.

20. *In a reducing salon:* Only 24 _____ days till Christmas.

Your Turn

Make up some punny signs for a laundry, a restaurant, a candy store, or any other place of business.

Answers to Riddles and Signs

Silly Billy jokes:

1. fly 2. fly 3. Giants 4. sleeping 5. smash hit

Elephant jokes:

6. In their trunks 7. Use a scoop of ice cream, some root beer, and an elephant. 8. It lets out a little whine. 9. Take away its credit card. 10. Harry Elephante and Elephant Gerald

Punny signs:

11. dry 12. star 13. false 14. Site 15. tock 16. time 17. pool 18. skid 19. bulbs 20. shaping

Homographs at Play

To a bowler, a _____ is knocking down all the pins.

After eating a meal at a restaurant, what did the duck say to the waiter?
"Put it on my bill."

What did Samson die of?
Fallen arches.

What is six feet long, green, and has two tongues?
The Jolly Green Giant's sneakers.

What is the favorite part of a road for a vampire?
The main artery.

Out on the ocean, a ship carrying red paint collided with another ship carrying blue paint. What happened to the crews?

They got marooned.

In each of these examples, the key words—*bill, arches, tongues, artery,* and *marooned*—spark forth two meanings:

In the first riddle, *bill* means both a statement of payment and a bird's nose.

In the second riddle, *arches* means both the curved support of a building and the curved support of a foot.

In the third riddle, *tongues* are parts of sneakers and parts of mouths.

In the fourth riddle, an *artery* is a main part of a highway and a main channel for blood.

In the fifth riddle, *marooned* means to be lost at sea and to be made purple.

Punning is largely the trick of packing two or more ideas into a single word or expression. Punning challenges us to apply the greatest pressure per square syllable of language. Punning surprises us by laughing at the law of nature that pretends that two things can't occupy the same space at the same time. Punning is an exercise of the mind at being concise.

The more we play with words, the more we find that most of them possess more than one meaning. Because words are alive, they refuse to sit still. As they grow older, they gather new meanings. Words wander wondrously.

The most basic form of punning springs from a single word that generates two or more different meanings. If those meanings spring from the same spelling, the pun is called a **homograph** (from the Greek, meaning "same writing"). A good pun is like a good steak—a rare medium well done!

Pun Fun

To sharpen your awareness of multiple meanings springing from a single spelling, try your hand and imagination at playing two games of homograph puns. After you have done your best, check the answers at the end of this chapter.

In each cluster of sentences below, identify the single word that can occupy each blank.

1. To a car owner, a _____ is a space for storage.

   To a zookeeper, a _____ is an elephant's appendage.

   To a forester, a _____ is the main support of a tree.

   To a doctor, a _____ is a human torso.

   To a traveler, a _____ is a portable box to put things in.

2. To a jeweler, a _____ is a circular band.

   To someone answering the telephone, a _____ is an audible signal.

   To a boxer, a _____ is an enclosure to fight in.

To an astronomer, a _____ is a circle of matter surrounding a heavenly body.

3. To most of us, a _____ is something at the end of our arm.

   To a ship's captain, a _____ is a crew member.

   To an entertainer, a _____ is a round of applause.

   To a clock maker, a _____ is a pointer on a dial.

   To a horse trainer, a _____ is a measurement of height.

To a ship's captain, a _____ is a crew member.

4. To a collector, a _____ is a number of things of the same kind.

   To a movie director, a _____ is the scene for a production.

   To a beautician, a _____ is an arrangement of hair.

   To a musician, a _____ is a session of music.

   To a tennis player, a _____ is a portion of a match.

5. To a baseball player, a _____ is a missed pitch.

   To a bowler, a _____ is knocking down all ten pins.

   To an employer, a _____ is a stopping of work on purpose.

   To a fisherman or fisherwoman, a _____ is a pull on the line.

   To a prospector, a _____ is a valuable discovery.

   To a play producer, a _____ is taking down a set.

Your Turn

List five words that have at least three meanings. Using those words, make up five homograph riddles.

Pun Fun

Now here's another game of fun with homographs. In each blank below, insert a word that means the same as the words that come before and after. The dashes indicate the number of letters in each missing word.

6. spinning toy __ __ __ summit

7. flying mammal __ __ __ baseball equipment

8. spheroid __ __ __ __ dance

9. gasps __ __ __ __ __ trousers

10. plunge __ __ __ __ season of the year

11. wound coil __ __ __ __ __ __ season of the year

12. strange __ __ __ not even

13. student __ __ __ __ __ part of the eye

14. whip __ __ __ __ part of the eye

15. remainder __ __ __ __ relaxation

16. deep hole ___ ___ ___ fruit stone

17. to close __ __ __ __ sea lion

18. playing area __ __ __ __ __ hall of justice

19. without cost __ __ __ __ liberate

20. coins __ __ __ __ __ __ alter

21. hurler __ __ __ __ __ __ __ container of liquid

22. even contest __ __ __ neckwear

23. king or queen __ __ __ __ __ measuring stick

24. jelly __ __ __ blockage

25. a flavor __ __ __ __ money factory

King or queen _ _ _ _ _ measuring stick.

Your Turn

Add five more questions to the list above. Quiz your classmates or friends.

Pun Fun

These days, if you ask people, "How's business?" they may answer you according to their profession.

"How's business?"
Pilot: "Up in the air."
Student: "It puts me to the test."
Plumber: "It's going down the drain."
Mountaineer: "Looking up."
Carpenter: "Groovy."
Restaurant owner: "It's from hunger."
Exterminator: "It's bugging me."
Elevator manufacturer: "It has its ups and downs."
Watch repairman: "Times are changing."
Skier: "It's all downhill from here."
Dietician: "Sometimes thick, sometimes thin."
Oil driller: "I'm getting in deeper and deeper."
Mint operator: "I'm making a lot of money."
Blacksmith: "I've got too many irons in the fire."

Your Turn

Make up another question that inspires at least five punny answers. Examples:

> How do you feel?
> How do I love thee?
> How's the weather?
> What's your favorite food?

"How do I love thee? Let me COUNT the ways."

Answers to Homographs

1. trunk 2. ring 3. hand 4. set 5. strike
6. top 7. bat 8. ball 9. pants 10. fall
11. spring 12. odd 13. pupil 14. lash 15. rest
16. pit 17. seal 18. court 19. free 20. change
21. pitcher 22. tie 23. ruler 24. jam 25. mint

Calling on the Homophone

*What do you
call an insect
relative?*

Perhaps the most popular of all children's riddles is "What's black and white and red (read)
all over? *A newspaper.*" Here the play of words is
on *red* and *read*, which sound the same but are
spelled differently.★

★This riddle is so well known that other answers have taken flight from it.
What's black and white and red (read) all over? *A penguin at Miami
Beach, a zebra with diaper rash, a skunk with measles, a nun who's spilled
ketchup on herself,* and *Santa Claus coming down the chimney.*

Many Americans grow up also reciting a version of this rhyme:

> *How much wood would a woodchuck chuck*
> *If a woodchuck could chuck wood?*
> *A woodchuck would chuck*
> *All the wood that a woodchuck could chuck*
> *If a woodchuck could chuck wood.*

The delight and popularity of this little verse can be explained by the lively rhythms, the clever rhyming of *woodchuck* and *could chuck*, and the pun on *woodchuck* and *would chuck*, which, again, sound the same but are spelled differently.

When two or more words are spelled differently but have the same sound, they are called **homophones** (from the Greek, meaning "same sound"). Here are examples of homophonic jokes:

Seven days without laughing make one weak.

A baker quit making doughnuts because he got tired of the hole business.

I'm on a seafood diet. Every time I see food, I eat it.

When the glassblower accidentally inhaled, he ended up with a pane in his stomach.

> *A tutor who tooted the flute*
> *Tried to tutor two tooters to toot.*
> *Said the two to the tutor,*
> *"Is it easier to toot or*
> *To tutor two tutors to toot?"*

In these homophonic riddles, the words with different spelling but identical sound are
weak and *week*
hole and *whole*
seafood and *see food*
pane and *pain*
to and *two, tutor* and *tooter*

Here are some rare triple plays that take delight with homophones:
A man gave his sons a cattle ranch and named it Focus because it was a spot where the sons raise meat.
                         the sun's rays meet.

A man was a successful perfume manufacturer. His business made a lot of sense.
                         scents.
                         cents.

Pun Fun

What do you call a naked grizzly?
    A bare bear.

Riddles like this are designed to open your eyes and ears to the joys of homophones. Each of the following clues should lead you to an answer consisting of two homophones. The first dozen items involve members of the animal kingdom.

What do you call

1. a pony with a sore throat?

2. a smelly chicken?

3. bunny fur?

4. an insect relative?

5. a cry from a large, sea–going mammal?

6. a fighting ape?

7. a precious buck?

8. a dragged cousin of the frog?

9. an inexpensive chick's cry?

10. smoked salmon's fastenings?

11. a recently acquired antelope?

12. an antlered animal's dessert?

Now try to come up with homophone pairs that do not involve animals.

What do you call a braver rock?
A bolder boulder.

What do you call

13. a late weekend ice-cream treat?

14. a wan bucket?

15. a simple, unadorned airliner?

16. a double sword fight?

17. dungarees for chromosomes?

18. a basement salesperson?

19. an entire burrow?

20. boat canvas bargains?

21. a sugary collection of rooms?

22. a hurled royal chair?

23. a spun globe?

24. a corridor on an island?

25. a conceited blood channel?

26. a young coal digger?

27. an odd marketplace?

28. unmoving writing paper?

29. an uninterested plank of wood?

30. a renter's boundary?

Your Turn

Make up five questions that begin with "What do you call?" Each answer should include a pair of homophones.

What do you call a braver rock?

Answers to Homophones

1. a hoarse horse 2. a foul fowl 3. hare hair
4. an ant aunt 5. a whale wail 6. a gorilla guerrilla
7. a dear deer 8. a towed toad 9. a cheap cheep
10. lox locks 11. a new gnu 12. moose mousse

13. a Sunday sundae 14. a pale pail 15. a plain plane
16. a dual duel 17. genes' jeans 18. a cellar seller
19. a whole hole 20. sails sales 21. a sweet suite
22. a thrown throne 23. a whirled world
24. an isle aisle 25. a vain vein 26. a minor miner
27. a bizarre bazaar 28. stationary stationery
29. a bored board 30. a boarder border

Double Plays **4**

Romance on the ocean: gull meets buoy.

In what direction does a sneeze travel?
Achoo!

What's the difference between the Prince of
Wales, an ape, and a bald–headed man?
*The Prince of Wales is the heir apparent. An ape
has a hairy parent. A bald–headed man has no
hair apparent.*

Upon discovering a new egg in the henhouse, the
excited chick chirped, "Marmalade a baby!"

Romance on the ocean: gull meets buoy.

Here's how to make a fortune. Buy fifty female pigs and fifty male deer. Then you'll have a hundred sows and bucks.

In homograph and homophone puns, one sound yields two meanings. In the examples that start this chapter, a slightly more complex process is at work. One sound generates two meanings, but the second meaning comes through a second sound that is phonetically related to the original sound.

That kind of play on words is called a **double sound pun**. Like homographs and homophones, double sound puns pack two or more meanings into a verbal space that they do not ordinarily occupy. Double sound puns are a truly rewording (rewarding) experience.

In the examples that start this chapter, the similar sounding words with different meanings are

achoo! and *at you*

heir apparent, hairy parent, and *hair apparent*

marmalade and *mamma laid*

gull and *girl* and *buoy* and *boy*

a hundred sows and bucks and *a hundred thousand bucks*

Pun Fun

Knock–knock jokes have been popular for almost a century. Many of us play the game as children and continue knock–knocking right through adulthood.

The punster says, "Knock, knock."

The second person replies, "Who's there?"

The knock–knocker comes back with something like "Dwayne."

"Dwayne who?" is the standard response.

The *pun*ch line is almost always a double sound pun, such as "Dwayne the bathtub; I'm dwowning." (Here the pun is on the name *Dwayne* and the word *drain*.)

Pun Fun

Knock, knock.
> *Who's there?*

Hair comb.
> *Hair comb who?*

Hair comb two games of knock–knock jokes.

Isadore and Isabel.

The first game plays on people's names. Match each name in the list below with the best *pun*ch line.

Knock, knock.

Who's there?   (Name) *Who?*

Adelle   1. _____ can you see?

Amos   2. _____ big dinner and got sick.

Andy   3. _____ dwops keep falling on my

Arthur   head.

Della   4. _____ my bubble gum.

Dexter   5. _____ catessen.

Harry   6. _____ is what a farmer lives in.

Henrietta   7. _____ locked?

Ira   8. _____ half as much as a dime.

Isabel   9. _____ quito bit me.

Isadore   10. _____ bit me again.

Ivan   11. _____ to be an actress.

Jose   12. _____ wall carpeting.

Lionel   13. _____ halls with boughs of holly.

Nicholas   14. _____ roar if you don't feed it.

Oliver   15. _____ the tub so I can take a

Oswald   bath.

Phillip   16. _____ up, we're late.

Walter   17. _____ mometer is broken.

Wayne   18. _____ member kindergarten.

               19. _____ out of order?

               20. _____ troubles will soon be over.

Knock, knock.
  Who's there?

Orange.
  Orange who?

Orange you glad there are more knock–knock jokes?

The second game plays upon words other than people's names. Match each word in the list below with the appropriate conclusion that follows:

aardvark

avenue

canoe

cheetahs

despair

doughnut

effervescent

event

eyewash

fangs

hence

hyena

ketchup

needle

omelette

ooze

radio

sofa

tuba

zombies

21. _____ to him before he gets away.

22. _____ not, here I come.

23. _____ afraid of the big bad wolf?

24. _____ help me with my homework?

25. _____ for helping me with my
homework.

26. _____ ever give up in life.

27. _____ never prosper.

28. _____ tire is flat.

29. _____ lay eggs.

30. _____ toothpaste

31. _____ smarter than I look.

32. _____ so good.

33. _____ make honey, and _____
don't.

34. _____ thataway!

35. _____ for books, I'd be bored.

36. _____ tree sat an owl.

37. _____ little money for the movies?

38. _____ is the key to success.

39. _____ you all the success in the
world.

40. _____ heard these jokes before?

Your Turn

Make up five knock–knock jokes. See if your friends or classmates can guess the *pun*chlines.

Answers to Knock–Knock Jokes

1. Jose 2. Henrietta 3. Wayne 4. Oswald 5. Della
6. Adelle 7. Isadore 8. Nicholas 9. Amos 10. Andy
11. Ivan 12. Walter 13. Dexter 14. Lionel 15. Phillip
16. Harry 17. Arthur 18. Ira 19. Isabel 20. Oliver
21. ketchup 22. radio 23. ooze 24. canoe 25. fangs
26. doughnut 27. cheetahs 28. despair 29. hence
30. tuba 31. omelette 32. sofa 33. zombies, zombies
34. event 35. effervescent 36. hyena 37. needle
38. aardvark 39. eyewash 40. avenue

Have You Ever Seen a Home Run?

What is wrong with each of these newspaper headlines?

EYE DROPS OFF SHELF

SQUAD HELPS DOG BITE VICTIM

CYPRESS FIGHTING MUSHROOMS

In each case, the headline can be read in two ways because of a confusion in the part of speech of one or more of the words.

In the first headline, are eyedrops now off the shelf, or did an eye drop off the shelf?

In the second headline, did the squad help a victim of a dog bite, or did the squad help the dog bite someone?

In the third headline, is Cypress fighting a bunch of mushrooms, or is the fighting in Cypress increasing?

CYPRESS FIGHTING MUSHROOMS.

The ability of many English words to change part of speech without changing shape produces not only a number of two-headed headlines, but also a bookful of riddles:

What has four wheels and flies?
　A garbage truck.

How do you make an elephant stew?
　Keep it waiting for two hours.

What did Silly Billy do when he came to a gas station with a sign that said, "Clean Rest Rooms"?
　He went inside and cleaned them.

The answers to these riddles rely on the fact that *flies, stew,* and *clean* are both nouns and verbs. The ease with which English words can move from noun to verb has inspired a game called "Have you ever seen?"
Have you ever seen
　a home run?
　a horse fly?
　a vegetable stand?
　a key ring?
　a pizza shop?
　a rock star?
　a mouse trap?
　a ski jump?

Pun Fun

Match the words in the left-hand column with the appropriate words in right-hand column.

Have you ever seen

1. a ball	bowl? dressing?
2. a belly	box? store? whistle?
3. a bull	chop?
4. a cat	clown?
5. a chair	cut?
6. a circus	dance?
7. an egg	dress? party?
8. a ginger	duck?
9. a hair	fence?
10. a jelly	fish? nap? nip?
11. a kitchen	fish? roll?
12. a lamb	dance? flop? laugh?
13. a peppermint	lift?
14. a picket	park?
15. a roast	plant? roll? shampoo?
16. a salad	ring? rush? whip?
17. a snow	shovel?
18. a square	sink?
19. a toy	snap?
20. a wedding	stick? twist?

**Have you ever seen a
square dance?**

Your Turn

Make up your own two–headed headlines or your own
riddles that use a shifted part of speech.

Make up five questions that begin with "Have you
ever seen?" The answers should each play with a shifted
part of speech.

Answers to "Have You Ever Seen?"

1. park? 2. dance? flop? laugh? 3. ring? rush? whip?
4. fish? nap? nip? 5. lift? 6. clown? 7. plant? roll?
shampoo? 8. snap? 9. cut? 10. fish? roll? 11. sink?
12. chop? 13. stick? twist? 14. fence? 15. duck?
16. bowl? dressing? 17. shovel? 18. dance? 19. box?
store? whistle? 20. dress? party?

Four Cheers Five Inflationary Language

A man wearing a four-piece suit and a threepee.

Many years ago, the pianist and comedian Victor Borge created the game of inflationary language. Since prices keep going up, Borge reasoned, why shouldn't language go up, too?

In the English language, there are words that contain the sounds of numbers, such as *wonder* (one), *before* (four), and *decorate* (eight). If we inflate each sound by one number, we come up with a string of puns—*twoder, befive,* and *decornine.*

Here is a story based on Borge's idea. This tale invites you to read and hear inflationary language in all its inflated wonder—oops, make that *twoder*. Try your eye and ear at translating the story into regular, uninflated English.

Jack and the Twoderful Beans

Twice upon a time there lived a boy named Jack in the twoderful land of Califivenia. Two day Jack, a double–minded lad, decided three go fifth three seek his fivetune.

After making sure that Jack nine a sandwich and drank some 8–Up, his mother elevenderly said, "Threedeloo, threedeloo. Try three be back by next Threesday." Then she cheered, "Three, five, seven, nine. Who do we apprecinine? Jack, Jack, yay!"

Jack set fifth and soon met a man wearing a four–piece suit and a threepee. Fifthrightly Jack asked the man, "I'm a Califivenian. Are you two three?"

"Cerelevenly," replied the man, offiving the high six. "Anytwo five elevennis?"

"Not threeday," answered Jack inelevently. "But can you help me three locnine my fivetune?"

"Sure," said the man. "Let me sell you these twoderful beans."

Jack's inthreeition told him that the man was a three–faced triple–crosser. Elevensely Jack shouted, "I'm not behind the nine ball. I'm a college gradunine, and I know what rights our fivefathers crenined in the

Constithreetion. Now let's get down three baseven about these beans."

The man tripled over with laughter. "Now hold on a third," he responded. "There's no need three make such a three–do about these beans. If you twot, I'll give them three you."

Well, there's no need three elabornine on the rest of the tale. Jack oned in on the giant and two the battle for the golden eggs. His mother and he lived happily fivever after—and so on, and so on, and so fifth.

Your Turn

List as many words as you can that contain the sounds of numbers. Then write an original story using a lot of inflationary language.

Deflating "Jack and the Twoderful Beans"

Jack and the Wonderful Beans

Once upon a time there lived a boy named Jack in the wonderful land of California. One day Jack, a single–minded lad, decided to go forth to seek his fortune.

After making sure that Jack ate a sandwich and drank some 7-Up, his mother tenderly said, "Toodeloo, toodeloo. Try to be back by next Tuesday." Then she cheered, "Two, four, six, eight. Who do we appreciate? Jack, Jack, yay!"

Jack set forth and soon met a man wearing a three–piece suit and a toupee. Forthrightly Jack asked the man, "I'm a Californian. Are you one too?"

"Certainly," replied the man, offering the high five. "Anyone for tennis?"

"Not today," answered Jack intensely. "But can you help me to locate my fortune?"

"Sure," said the man. "Let me sell you these wonderful beans."

Jack's intuition told him that the man was a two–faced double–crosser. Tensely Jack shouted, "I'm not behind the eight ball. I'm a college graduate, and I know what rights our forefathers created in the Constitution. Now let's get down to basics about these beans."

The man doubled over with laughter. "Now hold on a second," he responded. "There's no need to make such a to–do about these beans. If you want, I'll give them to you."

Well, there's no need to elaborate on the rest of the tale. Jack zeroed in on the giant and won the battle for the golden eggs. His mother and he lived happily forever after—and so on, and so on, and so forth.

"Let's Play a Game," Said Tom Swiftly

"I'm good with numbers," said Tom figuratively.

Almost a century ago, boys and girls grew up reading the adventures of Tom Swift. Young Tom was a sterling young hero who survived one scary experience after another while inventing everything from the motorcycle to the fax machine, from an electric airplane to a flying boat to a wizard camera. In the course of the heroic action, Tom and his friends and enemies never just said something; they always said it *excitedly* or *sadly* or *hurriedly*.

Tom Swift invented something else that he didn't even know about—a pun game. The object of the game is to match the adverb (the *–ly* word that describes the verb) with the quotation to produce, in each case, a clever pun:

"I want to be a doctor," said Tom patiently.

"I'm hoping to strike oil," said Tom boringly.

"I've struck oil," said Tom crudely.

"I love pancakes," said Tom flippantly.

"Rowing so much hurts my hands," said Tom callously.

"I've struck oil,"
said Tom crudely.

"I hate pineapples," said Tom dolefully.

"Let's go to McDonald's," said Tom archly.

"My glasses are fogged up," said Tom optimistically.

"Fire!" said Tom alarmingly.

"My radio's finally fixed," said Tom ecstatically.

"I'm good with numbers," said Tom figuratively.

"My cookie is empty," said Tom unfortunately.

"I love to go to the circus," said Tom intently.

"I hate fly fishing," said Tom downcastly.

"I'm going to kill Dracula," said Tom painstakingly.

"I love pancakes," said Tom flippantly.

Pun Fun

Now that you see how the Tom Swifty game works, match each statement in the left–hand column with the best swift adverb in the right–hand column.

1. "I'll have a hot dog."	crabbily
2. "My pencil is dull."	delightedly
3. "She tore my valentine in two."	frankly
	fruitlessly
4. "I can't find the apples."	grumpily
5. "I love getting caught in blackouts."	half–heartedly
	icily
6. "I'm a lion hunter."	ideally
7. "I flunked my exam."	listlessly
8. "Pass me the cards."	moodily
9. "Stop the horse!"	pointlessly
10. "I lost my shopping notes."	pridefully
	rapidly
11. "I'm one of the seven dwarfs."	testily
	woefully
12. "This river is rough."	
13. "Shall I frost the cake?"	
14. "I used to milk cows."	
15. "I hate shellfish."	

Your Turn

Make up five Tom Swifties. See if your friends or class-mates can guess the punny adverbs.

Swift Answers

1. frankly 2. pointlessly 3. half-heartedly 4. fruitlessly
5. delightedly 6. pridefully 7. testily 8. ideally
9. woefully 10. listlessly 11. grumpily 12. rapidly
13. icily 14. moodily 15. crabbily

A Bazaar Tail 8

This male wore mail for war.

Hears a rye peace eye maid up inn my idol thyme. Aye rote it four yew two sea Howe homophones Cannes seam sew whiled from there knows write too they're tows. With pried, eye no it will knot boar ewe. Its meant two bee red allowed:

> One night a knight on a hoarse horse
>   Rode out upon a road.
> This male wore mail for war and would
>   Explore a wood that glowed.

His tale I'll tell from head to tail.
I'll write his rite up right.
A hidden site our hero found,
A sight that I shall cite.

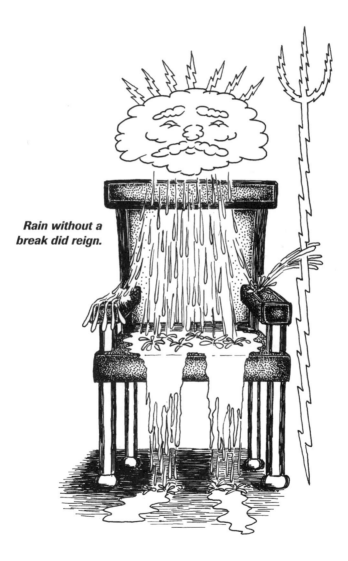

**Rain without a
break did reign.**

With woe he shouted, "Whoa!" as rain
Without a break did reign.
To brake, he pulled the rein, and like
A shattered pane, felt pain.

The poor knight met a witch, which made
Sweat pour from every pore.
He'd never seen a scene like that.
His sore heart couldn't soar.

Our knight began to reel, for real.
The world whirled, so to speak.
All the days of the week his sole soul felt
The dizzy daze of the weak.

Our heir to knighthood gave it up.
He felt the fare not fair.
His wholly holy sword soared up
As he threw it through the air.

The bell has tolled, I'm told. The hour
To end our tale draws nigh.
Without ado, I bid adieu,
So by your leave, bye–bye.

Pun Fun

List all the homophones that appear in the poem above and the paragraph that introduces it.

Your Turn

Make up a rhyming poem that contains at least four pairs of homophones.

A Bazaar Tail into A Bizarre Tale

First sentence: hears/here's, rye/wry, peace/piece, eye/I, maid/made, inn/in, idol/idle, thyme/time.

Second sentence: aye/I, rote/wrote, four/for, yew/you, two/to, sea/see, Howe/how, Cannes/can, seam/seem, sew/so, whiled/wild, there/their, knows/nose, write/right, too/to, they're/their, tows/toes.

Third sentence: pried/pride, eye/I, no/know, knot/not, boar/bore, ewe/you.

Fourth sentence: Its/it's, two/to, bee/be, red/read, allowed/aloud.

First stanza: night/knight, hoarse/horse, rode/road, male/mail, wore/war, would/wood.

Second stanza: tale/tail, write/rite/right, site/sight/cite.

Third stanza: woe/whoa!, rain/reign/rein, break/brake, pane/pain.

Fourth stanza: poor/pour/pore, witch/which, seen/scene, sore/soar.

Fifth stanza: reel/real, world/whirled, days/daze, sole/soul, week/weak.

Sixth stanza: heir/air, fare/fair, wholly/holy, sword/soared, threw/through.

Seventh stanza: tolled/told, hour/our, ado/adieu, by/bye–bye.

Licensed 2 Pun

It's fun to play around with the sounds of letters and numbers. Can you translate this classic dialogue, composed entirely of letters? Hint: the first line means "Have you any eggs?"

"F U NE X?"

"S, V F X."

"F U NE M?"

"S, V F M."

"OK, L F M N X."

Here's the translation:

"Have you any eggs?"

"Yes, we have eggs."

"Have you any ham?"

"Yes, we have ham."

"OK, I'll have ham and eggs."

Now try this mix of letters and numbers. Bear in mind that two of the same letter sounds like a plural. Thus, II means "eyes."

	Translation:
YURYY	Why you are wise
Is EZ 2 C	Is easy to see.
U UU your	You use your
XS NRG	Excess energy.
U XEd NE	You exceed any
MT TT.	Empty tease.
I NV how U	I envy how you
XL with EE	Excel with ease.

Pun Fun

According to recent surveys, more than two million Americans own vanity license plates. Instead of getting stuck with meaningless, preselected letter-number combinations, more and more car owners use the five or six allotted letters to create their own messages for their plates. Many of these licensed statements are revealing puns.

In the left-hand column below are ten authentic vanity license plates. Each plate announces, in a clever and compact way, the profession of the car owner. For example, a doctor's license plate reads YRUILL ("Why are you ill?").

Match each poetic license in the left-hand column with the corresponding profession in the right-hand column. RUREDY? GO4IT!

1. ADAM81	__ aerobics instructor
2. 4CAST	__ apple grower
3. IC2020	__ dairy farmer
4. IEDUC8	__ dentist
5. IOPER8	__ eye doctor
6. ISUM4U	__ lawyer
7. LOCMUP	__ police officer
8. MOOTEL	__ schoolteacher
9. 2THDR	__ surgeon
10. YRUFAT	__ weather person

Other personalized license plates convey a sense of identify or humor. Match each plate in the left-hand column with its creator in the right-hand column.

11. EIEIO   __ Chicago Cubs fan
12. 4CCUBS   __ farmer named McDonald
13. 2CTER   __ Miss Piggy fan
14. 10SNE1   __ sports car owner
15. XQQMOI   __ tennis player

Licentious Answers

1. apple grower 2. weatherperson 3. eye doctor
4. schoolteacher 5. surgeon 6. lawyer 7. police officer
8. dairy farmer 9. dentist 10. aerobics instructor
11. farmer named McDonald 12. Chicago Cubs fan
13. sports car owner 14. tennis player (tennis anyone?)
15. Miss Piggy fan (excuse moi)

Puns That Babylon

Maple I wood pine fir yew.

ne of the joys of punnery is to string categories of words into sentences that actually make punnishing sense. Here's a bird's-eye view of some fowl language:

Once upon a time there lived a raven-haired little gull named Robin. She hung around with a bunch of turkeys and cuckoos, but she was always happy as a lark. Although she sometimes was a chicken who quailed, she could be quite cocky. And, despite going on many a wild-goose chase, she was quite loosey-goosey and eagle-eyed. She always believed that ostrich in time saves nine and never had any egrets that her life was for the birds.

One, two, t'ree. Here's a little poem about two trees:

Maple I would pine fir yew.
Maple I would balsam tears.
My love for you is very larch
And evergreen will stay through years.

Once cypress yew against my heart,
Please say, "Oakay, I dew," dear miss.
Then we willow exchange our boughs
And live our lives in wooded bliss.

Your Turn

String together a bunch of puns into a paragraph using animals, fish, or any other part of nature as your theme.

Pun Fun

These days, we hear a lot about geographical illiteracy—the inability of students and grownups to name the capital of their particular state or to locate Vietnam on a world map. Here's a chance for you to increase your knowledge of geographical names as well as your skill in fabricating outrageous puns. I'm not kidding. I'm Syrias.

Use the list of countries and republics below to complete the statements that follow. Each item on the list appears only once in the answers, which you can find at the end of this chapter.

Belgium	Greece	Jamaica
Senegal	Bolivia	Haiti
Kenya	Spain	Brazil
Holland	Norway	Sudan
Chile	Hungary	Pakistan
Sweden	China	India
Panama	Tibet	Cuba
Iran	Poland	Turkey
Egypt	Iraq	Russia
Ukraine	France	Israel
Saudi	Uruguay	Germany
Wales		

1. Wear your winter coat today or you'll be _____.

2. Little Miss Muffet liked neither curds _____.

3. Save the _____ before they become extinct.

4. Not only did Frank gyp you, _____ me.

5. I'm a gal and _____.

6. I've never _____ like you.

7. I can't figure out what's causing thi _____ in my arm.

8. Please _____ board in two.

9. My back pack is dark brown, but your back _____.

10. With _____ like these, who needs enemies?

11. You stood here, but _____.

12. Iran is a country between _____ and a hard place.

13. The sun will come up when it comes up. You can't _____ sunrise.

14. I wonder what's gotten _____.

15. A strong antibody will win over a _____ time.

16. I see that your little sister is taking piano lessons. _____ do it?

17. I love orange juice, but I _____.

18. If you can pan a pa, I can _____.

19. My zebra's healthy, but your ze_____.

20. Alco_____ cigarettes are bad habits.

21. Dan's car plowed into mine, so I'm going to _____.

22. Hey, Jim. _____ ring the _____?

23. If _____ your neck, you'll see that her medal is fake, but my hair _____.

24. Give me a good _____ I'll be willing _____ that I can vault fifteen feet.

25. I don't _____ broke my _____ vase.

26. Dad uses a _____ sugar to _____ his coffee.

27. On Thanksgiving, I get _____ for _____, if it doesn't have too much _____.

Your Turn

"What did Delaware? She wore a New Jersey," sang the words to a popular song of many years ago. Create a state-of-the-art game or poem that uses the names of the United States as puns.

Answers

1. Chile 2. Norway 3. Wales 4. Egypt 5. Uruguay
6. Senegal 7. Spain 8. Saudi 9. Pakistan 10. France
11. Iran 12. Iraq 13. Russia 14. India 15. Germany
16. Jamaica 17. Haiti 18. Panama 19. Brazil
20. Holland 21. Sudan 22. Kenya, Belgium
23. Ukraine, Israel 24. Poland, Tibet 25. Bolivia,
China 26. Cuba, Sweden 27. Hungary, Turkey, Greece

Pun Your Way to Success

Of all the things you wear, your expression is the most important.

t's worth repeating that a good pun is like a good steak—a rare medium well done. Before you start beefing about my spare ribbing, remember that many a meaty pun has been cooked up as advice on how to succeed in life.

Here is some punderful advice that merits a blue ribbin'. Sharpen your pun cells and start taking notes. Many of these puns can help you to climb the ladder of success in life without getting rung out. Let's get right to wit:

The difference between a champ and a chump is U.

Triumph is just umph added to try.

The only place where success comes before work is the dictionary.

The best vitamin for making friends is B–1.

Patience is counting down without blasting off.

Patience requires a lot of wait.

You can have an open mind without having a hole in your head.

She who throws mud loses ground.

If the going gets easy, you may be going downhill.

If you must cry over spilled milk, please try to condense it.

Failure is the past of least persistence.

Life is not so much a matter of position as disposition.

Success is more attitude than aptitude.

Our favorite attitude should be gratitude.

Of all the things you wear, your expression is the most important.

If at first you don't succeed, try, try a grin.

People who never make a mistake never make anything else.

When you feel yourself turning green with envy, you're ripe to be plucked.

She who throws mud loses ground.

There's nothing in the middle of the road but yellow stripes and dead armadillos.

There are two finishes for automobiles—lacquer and liquor.

He who laughs, lasts.

Pun Fun

Here are fifteen more punny slogans. Supply the missing words.

1. When the going gets tough, the tough get
   _____.

2. Hard work is the yeast that raises the _____.

3. Minds are like parachutes: they function only
   when _____.

4. Break a bad habit—_____ it.

5. To keep your mind clean and healthy, _____
   it once in a while.

6. One thing you can give and still keep is your
   _____.

7. A smile doesn't cost a cent, but it gains a lot of
   _____.

8. Learn that the bitter can lead to the _____.

9. Fear is the darkroom where _____ are
   developed.

10. Don't learn safety rules by _____.

Even though it's a jungle out there, a collection of
beastly puns may help you succeed in the world. Here
are some finny lines that you can't carp about, even if
you're hard of herring.

11. If you behave more like a chimp than a champ,
    you'll make a _____ out of yourself.

12. Frogs have it easy. They can eat what _____
    them.

13. A turtle makes progress when it sticks its
_____ out.

14. Birds have _____ too, but they keep on
singing.

15. Be like the woodpecker. Just keep pecking away
until you finish the job. You'll succeed by using
your _____.

Your Turn

Create your own lessons for life that employ puns to
put across your point.

Answers to Punny Slogans

1. going 2. dough 3. open 4. drop 5. change
6. word 7. interest 8. better 9. negatives 10. accident
11. monkey 12. bugs 13. neck 14. bills 15. head

A Daffynitions Fictionary

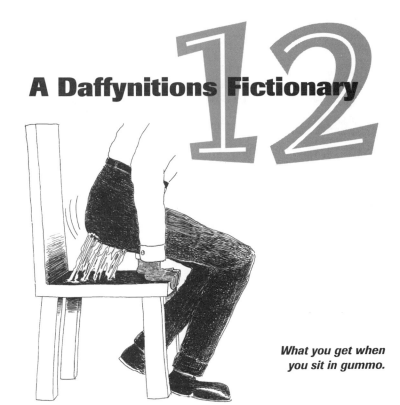

What you get when you sit in gummo.

Some playful genius once defined *khakis* as "what you need to start your automobile," and another verbathlete defined a *buccaneer* as "the cost of a two-dollar pair of earrings." Punderful definitions like these take a fresh approach to the sounds of old words. You won't find such entries in dictionaries, only in fictionaries, but they do have a name—daffynitions.

Here are ten of the daffiest daffynitions ever punned:

alarms. What an octopus is.

coffee. Snow White's eighth dwarf; Sneezy's younger brother.

forfeit. What most animals stand on.

fungi. The life of the party.

hootenanny. Sounds made when an owl flies smack into a goat.

pasteurize. Too far to see.

shampoo. A fake bear.

stucco. What you get when you sit in gummo.

toboggan. What you go to an auction for.

vitamin. What you do when guests come to your house.

What a hen will do with an egg.

Pun Fun

Figuring out and creating your own daffynitions exercises your verbal muscles. Match each entry below with the best daffynition in the list:

announce
appeal
benign
camelot
dandelion
fodder
hatchet
kidney
microwave
yellow

1. What a hen will do with an egg.
2. What you do when you step on a tack.
3. A swell king of the jungle.
4. A small goodbye.
5. One sixteenth of a pound.
6. What we wish when we're eight.
7. What a banana comes in.
8. Parking area for humped animals.
9. Married to da mudder.
10. Child's joint.

A small goodbye.

Your Turn

Now you are ready to make up your own daffynitions. Here are ten words for you to define punderfully:

11. bacteria

12. detour

13. goblet

14. illegal

15. locomotive

16. moon

17. peekaboo

18. specimen

19. tulips

20. zinc

Answers to Daffynitions

1. hatchet 2. yellow 3. dandelion 4. microwave
5. announce 6. benign 7. appeal 8. camelot
9. fodder 10. kidney

Each of the following daffynitions is but one of a number of possible answers:

11. where they serve germs 12. what we take in da museum 13. a young turkey 14. a sick bird
15. a crazy train 16. what cows are always doin'
17. hide and seek for ghosts 18. astronauts 19. frames for the mouth 20. where you wash your face

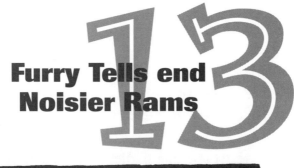

Furry Tells end Noisier Rams

Ladle Rat Rotten Hut.

adle rat rotten hut. What do these four words mean to you? Most likely they seem to you to be a random listing of four unrelated words. But try saying the list aloud, stressing the first and third words. Aha! Out comes something that sounds amazingly like "little red riding hood."

This kind of spectacular double-sound punning is the topsy turvy stuff of *Anguish Languish* ("English Language") by Howard L. Chace. In *Anguish Languish*, Professor Chace offers giltteringly new versions of furry tells ("fairy tales") and noisier rams ("nursery rhymes"). In each example, Chace replaces all the words in the original version with words that are similar but never quite the same in sound.

Here, for example, is the opening paragraph of the furry tell "Ladle Rat Rotten Hut":

Wants pawn term, dare worsted ladle gull hoe lift wetter mortar inner ladle cord age honor itch offer lodge, dock florist. Disk ladle gull orphan worry ladle cluck wetter putty ladle rat hut, end fur disk raisin pimple colder "Ladle Rat Rotten Hut."

Here is the translation of the paragraph into English Language:

Once upon a time, there was a little girl who lived with her mother in a little cottage on the edge of a large, dark forest. This little girl often wore a little cloak with her pretty little red hat, and for this reason people called her "Little Red Riding Hood."

Oriole ratty? Den less gut stuttered! In English Language that means: "Are we all ready? Then let's get started!"

Try translating the openings of two more furry tells.

Guilty Looks Enter Tree Boars

Wants pawn term dare worsted ladle gull how hat search putty yowler coils debt pimple colder Guilty Looks. Guilty Looks lift inner ladle cord age neck stew a beg florist, any ladle gull orphan aster mortar toe ladder goo tidy florist oil buyer shelf.

Guilty Looks.

Center Alley

Center Alley worse jester par ladle gull how loft wetter stop-mortar and toe heft cisterns. Daze worming war furry wicket and shellfish parsons. Oily inner moaning day wicket oiled worming shorted, "Center Alley, Center Alley, yo lacy ladle bomb! Gut otter bet and gutter irk!" Nor wander purr Center Alley worse tarred an disgorged.

What are your interpretations of these Noisier Rams?

Marry Hatter Ladle Limb

Marry hatter ladle limb.
Itch fleas worse widest snore.
An ever war debt Marry win
Door limb worse shorter gore.

Oiled Mortar Harbored

Oiled Mortar Harbored
Win tooter cardboard
Tow gutter pair darker boon.
Wind sheet gut dare,
Duck cardboard worse blare,
End soda pair dark hat noon.

Pitter Paper

Pitter Paper peeked uh packer pimpled poppers.
Uh packer pimpled poppers Pitter Paper peeked.
Oaf Pitter Paper peeked uh packer pimpled poppers,
Ware author pimpled poppers dot Pitter Paper peeked?

Your Turn

Write an Anguish Languish version of a furry tell or noisier ram of your choice. All the words must be different from the words in the original tale or rhyme. Have fun reading your creation aloud. Ask your classmates or friends to translate your Anguish Languish version into English Language.

Furry Tells end Noisier Rams into Fairy Tales and Nursery Rhymes

Goldie Locks and the Three Bears

Once upon a time there was a little girl who had such pretty yellow curls that people called her Goldie Locks. Goldie Locks lived in a little cottage next to a big forest, and the little girl often asked her mother to let her go to the forest all by herself.

Cinderella

Cinderella was just a poor little girl who lived with her stepmother and two half sisters. These women were very wicked and selfish persons. Early in the morning the wicked old woman shouted, "Cinderella, Cinderella, you lazy little bum! Get out of bed and get to work!" No wonder poor Cinderella was tired and discouraged.

Mary Had a Little Lamb

Mary had a little lamb.
Its fleece was white as snow.
And everywhere that Mary went
The lamb was sure to go.

Old Mother Hubbard

Old Mother Hubbard
Went to the cupboard
To get her poor dog a bone.
When she got there,
The cupboard was bare,
And so the poor dog had none.

Peter Piper

Peter Piper picked a peck of pickled peppers.
A peck of pickled peppers Peter Piper picked.
If Peter Piper picked a peck of pickled peppers,
Where are the pickled peppers that Peter Piper picked?

Silver Spoonerisms

"Ye noble tons of soil."

Perhaps you know somebody—and that somebody could be you—who occasionally says
pascetti for *spaghetti, aminal* for *animal,* and *reve-
lant* for *relevant.* Each of these mispronunciations
indicates a tendency to anticipate and, hence, to switch
sounds between words.

When such a transposition becomes comic, we call it
a spoonerism, named after the Rev. William Archibald
Spooner (1844–1930), dean and later warden (presi-
dent) of New College, Oxford, in England. He was a
distinguished professor, but he was best known around

the yards of Oxford for his hilarious slips of the tongue that became tips of the slung. Born with a silver spoonerism in his mouth, William Archibald Spooner set out to become a bird-watcher but ended up instead as a word botcher.

"Did you hear the latest spoonerism?" Oxford wits would ask one another. In this manner, Spooner entered the immortal company of Charles C. Boycott, the Earl of Sandwich, and Amelia Jenks Bloomer, who have had their names enshrined in our vocabulary.

The first of Spooner's spoonerisms, and one of the few that has been authenticated, was spoken by the great man in 1879, when he was conducting a service and announced the hymn as "Kinkering Kongs Their Titles Take." Perhaps his most famous switch occurred when, while lifting a tankard of ale to Queen Victoria, he bellowed, "Three cheers for our queer old dean!"

Seeing a woman parishioner in his space in church, he is said to have said, "Mardon me padam, you are occupewing my pie, may I sew you to another sheet?"

Yet another Spooner classic has him scolding a misbehaving student thusly: "You have hissed all my mystery lectures. You have tasted a whole worm. Please leave Oxford on the next town drain."

Here are some more tongue tangles attributed to Spooner:

Officiating at a wedding, he informed the groom that "it is kisstomary to cuss the bride."

He attended a naval review and marveled at the vast display of "cattleships and bruisers."

After dropping his hat, he asked, "Will nobody pat my hiccup?"

He told a gathering of patriots during World War I, "When the boys come home from France, we'll have the hags flung out."

Paying a visit to a school official, he asked, "Is the bean dizzy?"

He addressed a group of farmers as "Ye noble tons of soil."

Whether or not Spooner spoonerized as creatively and hilariously as in the above examples, spoonerizing has been raised to the highest level of verbal art. In presenting some of the best examples, we can identify three basic categories of spoonerisms. The most common is to switch initial consonants:

One blackbird to another: Bred any good rooks lately?

Psychologist: a person who pulls habits out of rats.

Combined charity drives put all the begs in one ask–it.

An ancient jungle king tyrannized his subjects and forced them to build him one elaborate throne after another—first of mud, then bamboo, then tin, then copper, then silver and so on. When the king became tired of each throne, he would store it in the attic of his grass hut. One day the attic collapsed, and the thrones crashed down upon the chief's head and killed him.

The moral of the tale is: People who live in grass houses shouldn't stow thrones.

A second popular type of spoonerizing is the reversal of syllables:

A good masseur leaves no stern untoned.

A man who hated seabirds left no tern unstoned.

A baker invented a special multibladed cutting instrument and called it a four–loaf cleaver.

I'd rather have a bottle in front of me than a frontal lobotomy.

A fisherman carelessly dropped his wallet into the water and was amazed to see a school of carp deftly balancing the wallet on their noses ands tossing it from one fish to the other. "Gosh," exclaimed the fisherman, "That's the first time I've ever seen carp to carp walleting!"

A four-loaf cleaver.

A stout woman entered a room, and an elderly gentleman did not rise. She was not amused and huffed at him, "Well, I see you're not so gallant as when you were a boy."

He shot right back, "And I see that you're not so buoyant as when you were a gal!"

Finally, we create spoonerisms by transposing whole words:

What's the difference between a cat and a comma? One has claws at the end of its paws, while the other has pause at the end of its clause.

Invention is the mother of necessity.

Time wounds all heels.

A critic said that he never panned the opening show of a new theater season because he didn't want to stone the first cast.

Slogan for a radio news team: No sooner done than said.

A bunch of cattle put into a satellite was called the herd shot round the world.

Those of us on eternal diets know that a waist is a terrible thing to mind.

A cannibal gave his wife for her birthday a box of Farmer's Fannies.

In days of old when knights were bold, people were a lot smaller than they are today— so much smaller, in fact, that many knights rode upon large dogs when they couldn't get horses.

One dark and stormy night, as the rain blew about, a squire entered a pet store in order to purchase a large dog for his master, the Black Knight.

Unfortunately, all the shopkeeper could offer the squire was one undersized, mangy mutt.

Commented the squire: "I wouldn't send a knight out on a dog like this!"

The English language is specially designed for spoonerizing. Because our language boasts far more words than any other—more than 615,000, compared to German, in second place with 185,000—we have far more rhyming words and, hence, more spoonerisms.

Take any two words and switch their order, and you will find that at least one of the two new words has meaning—a *ghost town* becomes a *toast gown,* a *toll booth* becomes a *bowl tooth,* and a *butterfly* becomes a *flutterby.* In remembering William Archibald Spooner, we celebrate the whiz and witdom of our English language.

Have you found this little essay on spoonerisms to be a truly re–wording experience? Good. As one frog said to another, "Time's fun when you're having flies!"

What's the Difference?

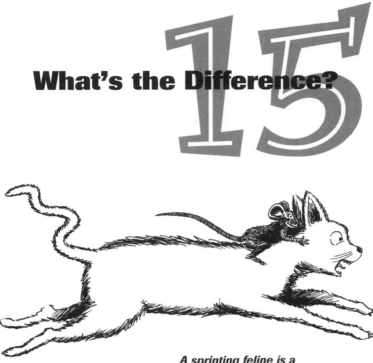

A sprinting feline is a _____ _____.
A clever rodent is a _____ _____.

Many English-speaking children first learn how to spoonerize by hearing and posing a special kind of riddle that begins with the formula "What's the difference?"

What's the difference between a pursued deer and an undersized witch?

One is a hunted stag; the other is a stunted hag.

What's the difference between a church bell and a thief?

One peals from the steeple; the other steals from the people.

What's the difference between a mouse and a pretty girl?

One harms the cheese; the other charms the he's.

What's the difference between an oak tree and a tight shoe?

One makes acorns; the other makes corns ache.

A jumping sorcerer is a _____ _____.
A crying reptile is a _____ _____.

Pun Fun

Now it's time for you to splay a pame of goonerisms—oops, I mean play a game of spoonerisms. Using the clues provided, fill in the blanks to complete each spoonerized expression. I guarantee that this exercise will warm your mart and hind and tickle your bunny phone. Oh, oh, I mean your heart and mind and funny bone.

1. A fisherman baits his _____.
   A lazy schoolboy _____ his _____.

2. A chimp holding on to a branch is a dangling _____.

   A destructive mule is a _____ _____.

3. Rotten lettuce makes a bad _____.
   A depressing song is a _____ _____.

4. If you like books, you have a reading _____.
   A prudent bunny is a _____ _____.

5. A tube is a hollow _____.
   A crazy Dutchman is a _____ _____.

6. A dentist yanks for the _____.
   A New York baseball fan _____ for the

   _____.

7. A swift cyclist is a speeding _____.
   A book-loving web-spinner is a _____ _____.

8. Sacks of coins are _____ _____.
   Rabbit periodicals are bunny _____.

9. A well-brushed equine is a curried _____.
   Rapid teaching makes for a _____ _____.

10. Thomas' English Muffins have nooks and

    _____.

    Thieves and governesses are _____ and

    _____.

11. Rabbit fur is _____ _____.
    A sweet-toothed grizzly is a _____ _____.

12. An adorable glove is a _____ _____.
    A silent baby cat is a _____ _____.

13. A sprinting feline is a _____ _____.
    A clever rodent is a _____ _____.

14. Chilly lasses are _____ _____.
    Blonde ringlets are _____ _____.

15. A large needle is a _____ _____.
    Hogs eat out of a _____ _____.

16. A jumping sorcerer is a _____ _____.
    A crying reptile is a _____ _____.

17. Dark cows and bulls are _____ _____.
    A war for the throne is a _____ _____.

18. A jammed entrance is a _____ _____.
    A place that sells quackers is a _____ _____.

19. An unwelcome party guest is a _____ _____.
    One who breaks boxes is a _____ _____.

20. Two pairs of hosiery are _____ _____.
    A hurting vulpine is a _____ _____.

Your Turn

Make up five original "What's the difference?" riddles. Have your classmates or friends try to guess the answers.

Answers to "What's the Difference?"

1. baits his hook/hates his book
2. dangling monkey/mangling donkey
3. bad salad/sad ballad
4. reading habit/heeding rabbit
5. hollow cylinder/silly Hollander
6. yanks for the roots/roots for the Yanks
7. speeding rider/reading spider
8. money bags/bunny mags
9. curried horse/hurried course
10. nooks and crannies/crooks and nannies
11. bunny hair/honey bear
12. cute mitten/mute kitten
13. running cat/cunning rat
14. cold girls/gold curls
15. big pin/pig bin
16. leaping wizard/weeping lizard
17. brown cattle/crown battle
18. stuck door/duck store
19. gate crasher/crate gasher
20. four socks/sore fox

Tairy Fales 16

Beeping Slooty.

Among the most sparkling examples of spoonerisms are those concocted by Frederick Chase Taylor. Better known as Colonel Lemuel Q. Stoopnagle, of the 1930s Stoopnagle and Budd CBS radio team, Taylor was a master of the "tairy fale." Here are versions of two of his best tongue tanglers:

Beeping Slooty

Tonce upon a wime, there lived a proxy fincess. When she was a bee waby, food gairies gave her a bunning stooty and wait grisdom. Then a fad bairy said that when she tweached her bentieth rirthday, she would frick her pinger on a prindle. But the food gairy said that when she fricked her pinger, she would only doll into a seep fleep. Levertheness, her caddy the ding was vorely sexed and had all the winning spiels in the bingdom kurned.

Well, when the fruitable bincess tweached the rage of enty, she was pandering round the walace and came upon a wugly old itch spitting and sinning. When she spied the trindle, she fricked her pinger and, wick as a quink, dell into a seep fleep. When she did, all the portiers in the callous sell afleep too, and outside a horny gredge threw up.

Pime tassed, and no one could thenetrate the porns. Then a hung and prancesome yince came biding rye. At a futch of his tinger, the horny pedge tharted. When the yince saw Beeping Slooty, he hissed ler on the kips, and immediately, she smoke up and wiled. They were parried in the malace and hived lappily ever after.

Prinderella and the Cince

Tonce upon a wime, there lived a gritty little pearl named Prinderella. She lived with her sticked wepmother and her sugly isters. They made her pine all the shots and shans, wean all the clindows, and do all the wirty dirk around the house.

98

Isn't that a shirty dame?

Isn't that a shirty dame?

One day the ping issued a croclamation that all the geligible irls in the kingdom should come to a drancy fess ball. Prinderella didn't have a drancy fess. All she had was an irty drag.

Isn't that a shirty dame?

So off went the sticked wepmother and the three sugly isters to the drancy fess ball while Prinderella stayed home, and who should appear but Prinderella's gairy fodmother. Well, the gairy fodmother quickly turned a cumpkin into a poach, four hice into morses, and Prinderella's irty drag into a dragnificent mess with a stink mole. And she said, "Now, Prinderella, you go off to the drancy fess ball and have a tood gime—but you must be home by the moke of stridnight or the brell will be spoken!"

The moke of stridnight—such a shirty dame.

So off went Prinderella to the drancy fess ball, and she did have a tood gime there because she met a pransome hince. She pranced with the dince all light nong and was pickled tink. But, at the moke of stridnight, Prinderella ran down the stalace peps, and do you know what she did?

She slopped her dripper.

Such a shirty dame.

The next day, the ping issued another croclamation that all the geligible irls in the kingdom should sly on the tripper. The sticked wepmother slied on the tripper, but it fidn't did. The three sugly isters slied on the tripper, but it fidn't did. But Prinderella flipped her soot into the tripper—and it fid did!

So she and the dince mot garried, and they hived lappily ever after.

And the storal of the mory is: If you want to harry a prancesome mince, be sure to slop your dripper.

Your Turn

Create your own spoonerized version of a fairy tale or famous story or poem. Try to include a number of reversals that contain meaning. Have fun reading your creation aloud. Ask your classmates friends to translate your spoonerized words and expressions into normal English.